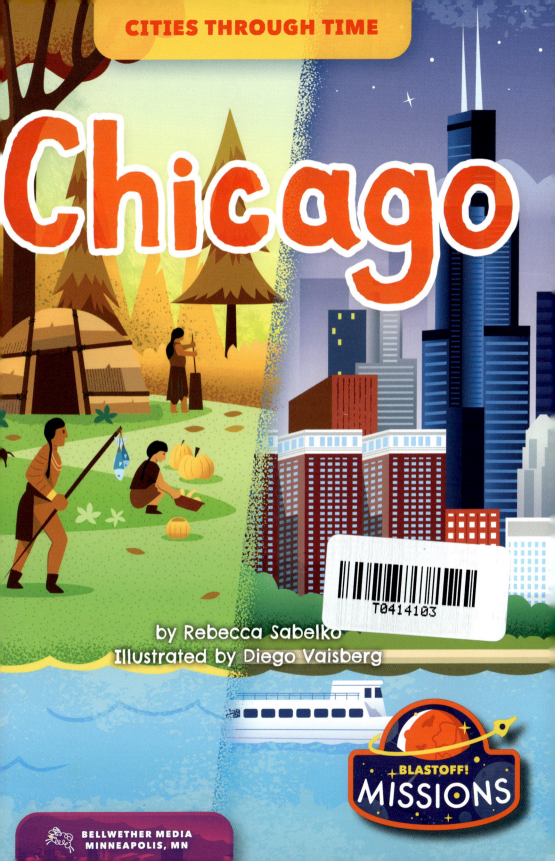

Chicago

by Rebecca Sabelko
Illustrated by Diego Vaisberg

T0414103

BLASTOFF!
MISSIONS

BELLWETHER MEDIA
MINNEAPOLIS, MN

Blastoff! Missions takes you on a learning adventure! Colorful illustrations and exciting narratives highlight cool facts about our world and beyond. Read the mission goals and follow the narrative to gain knowledge, build reading skills, and have fun!

Traditional Nonfiction

Narrative Nonfiction

Blastoff! Universe

MISSION GOALS

> FIND YOUR SIGHT WORDS IN THE BOOK.

> LEARN ABOUT DIFFERENT PERIODS IN CHICAGO'S HISTORY.

> LEARN ABOUT EVENTS THAT HELPED CHICAGO GROW.

This edition first published in 2025 by Bellwether Media, Inc.

No part of this publication may be reproduced in whole or in part without written permission of the publisher. For information regarding permission, write to Bellwether Media, Inc., Attention: Permissions Department, 6012 Blue Circle Drive, Minnetonka, MN 55343.

Library of Congress Cataloging-in-Publication Data

Names: Sabelko, Rebecca, author. | Vaisberg, Diego, illustrator.
Title: Chicago / by Rebecca Sabelko ; [illustrated by Diego Vaisberg].
Description: Minneapolis, MN : Bellwether Media, Inc., 2025. | Series: Blastoff! Missions: Cities Through Time | Includes bibliographical references and index. | Audience: Ages 5-8 | Audience: Grades 2-3 | Summary: "Vibrant illustrations accompany information about the history of Chicago. The narrative nonfiction text is intended for students in kindergarten through third grade." -Provided by publisher.
Identifiers: LCCN 2024021458 (print) | LCCN 2024021459 (ebook) | ISBN 9798886870015 (library binding) | ISBN 9798893041392 (paperback) | ISBN 9781644878385 (ebook)
Subjects: LCSH: Chicago (Ill.)--History--Juvenile literature.
Classification: LCC F548.33 .S23 2025 (print) | LCC F548.33 (ebook) | DDC 977.3/11--dc23/eng/20240517
LC record available at https://lccn.loc.gov/2024021458
LC ebook record available at https://lccn.loc.gov/2024021459

Editor: Christina Leaf   Designer: Laura Sowers

Printed in the United States of America, North Mankato, MN.

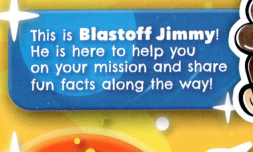

This is **Blastoff Jimmy**! He is here to help you on your mission and share fun facts along the way!

Table of Contents

Welcome to Chicago!

Here we are in Chicago, Illinois. It is a major city in the United States. Nearly three million people live here!

How did it become the **diverse** city it is today?

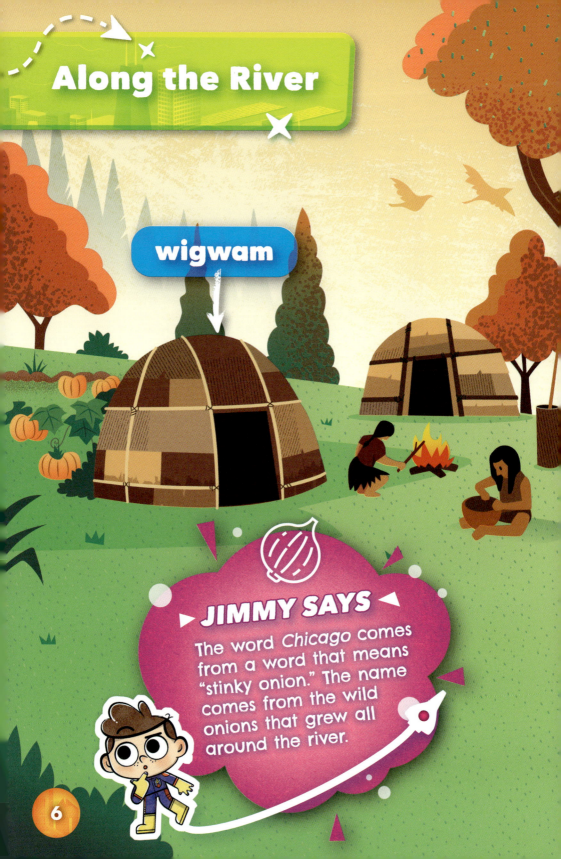

wigwam

▶ **JIMMY SAYS** ◀

The word *Chicago* comes from a word that means "stinky onion." The name comes from the wild onions that grew all around the river.

6

Let's paddle up the Chicago River. A Potawatomi village sits along the bank.

These people are preparing for winter. Their **wigwams** will keep them warm.

Chicago River

wild onions

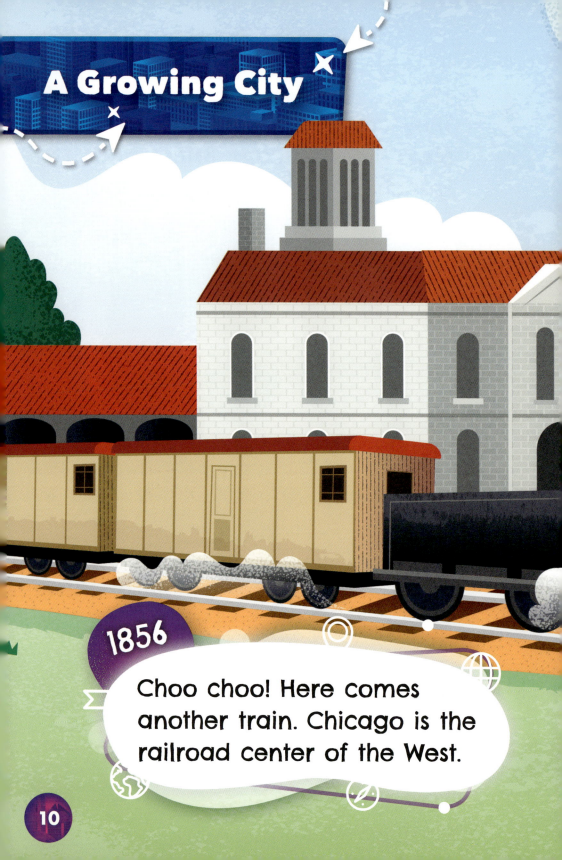

1856

Choo choo! Here comes another train. Chicago is the railroad center of the West.

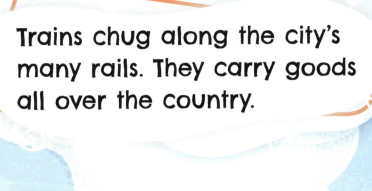

Trains chug along the city's many rails. They carry goods all over the country.

1871

Chicago is on fire! Winds sweep the flames from block to block.

The city's wooden streets, sidewalks, and buildings burn to the ground. Can the people rebuild the city?

12

JIMMY SAYS

Nearly 100,000 people lost their homes during the Great Chicago Fire of 1871.

14

1893

Welcome to the World's Fair! People from around the world are here to see new inventions.

Let's ride the Ferris Wheel. It goes so high! We can see over Lake Michigan.

These people go to work in the city's factories. They are some of the many Black people who moved here from the South.

In time, their communities will create great businesses, music, and art.

mid-1970s

Get ready to land at O'Hare **International** Airport. It is an important **airline hub**.

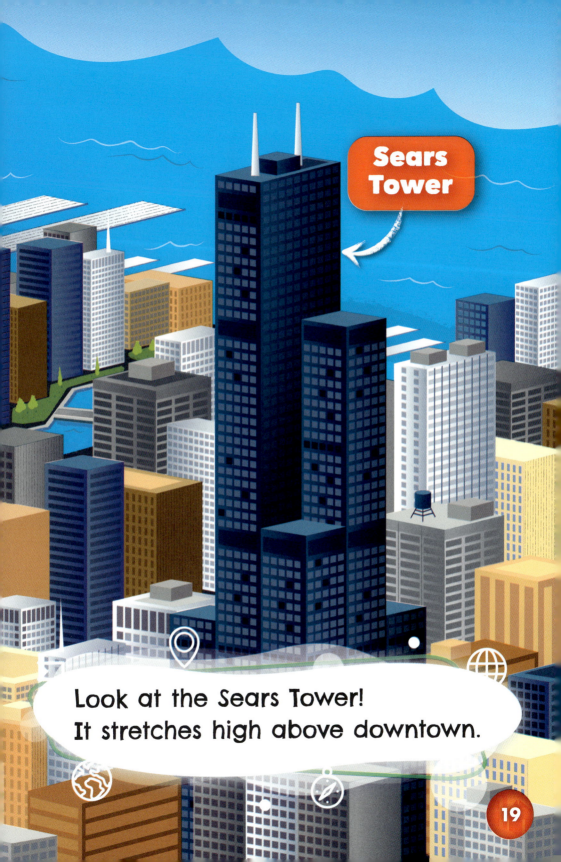

Sears
Tower

Look at the Sears Tower!
It stretches high above downtown.

19

The City Today

today

People explore Chicago's museums and neighborhoods. They check out shows and restaurants.

Chicago's many changes made the city what it is today!

Chicago Timeline

late 1600s: The Potawatomi live along the Chicago River

around 1779: Jean Baptiste Point DuSable opens a trading post and becomes the first settler of Chicago

1856: Chicago is the railroad center of the West

1871: The Great Chicago Fire burns much of the city

1893: Chicago hosts the World's Fair

1915 to 1940: Many Black people move from the South to northern cities like Chicago

mid-1970s: O'Hare International Airport becomes an airline hub and the Sears Tower, today's Willis Tower, is completed

Chicago, U.S.A.

Glossary

airline hub–an airport that is used by one or more airlines; airline hubs are connection points that help people get to their final travel spots.

diverse–made up of people from many different backgrounds

explorers–people who travel through a place in order to learn more about it or find something

international–related to the world

native–originally from a certain place

trading post–a place far from cities or towns where goods and services can be traded

wigwams–homes made of bark or animal furs covering a structure of wooden poles

To Learn More

AT THE LIBRARY

Leaf, Christina. *New York City*. Minneapolis, Minn.: Bellwether Media, 2024.

Rathburn, Betsy. *A Train's Day*. Minneapolis, Minn.: Bellwether Media, 2024.

Rudolph, Jessica. *Chicago*. New York, N.Y.: Bearport Publishing, 2018.

ON THE WEB

FACTSURFER

Factsurfer.com gives you a safe, fun way to find more information.

1. Go to www.factsurfer.com.

2. Enter "Chicago" into the search box and click 🔍.

3. Select your book cover to see a list of related content.

BEYOND THE MISSION

> WHAT FACT FROM THE BOOK DID YOU THINK WAS THE MOST INTERESTING?

> WHICH POINT IN CHICAGO'S HISTORY WOULD YOU WANT TO VISIT? WHY?

> DRAW A PICTURE OF WHAT YOU THINK CHICAGO WILL LOOK LIKE IN THE FUTURE.

Index